Women and Other Catastrophes
By Rashad Hawkins

To

Minnie Hawkins

I love you and I miss you so much.

Acknowledgements:

I have a lot of people to thank but I'll make an effort to be as brief as I can. First off to God, thank you for making all of these words knock on the door of my brain. Second, to my mother Serena, for always pushing me, believing in me, and for never shutting up about how many poems I had every day. To everyone else, from my father, Terry for passing his gift of prose to me. To Rick, Aaron, Dhante, Kierra, Jasmyne, Louis, Rasean, Santana, Brittney, Roro, Rebecca, Tisha, Gabrielle, Tashima, Jawayne, Grandma Minnie, Tonya, AJ, Mrs. Jones, Mr. Moon, Mr. Napier, Christini, Shakura, Chris, Ahmed, Brandon, Mr. Jackson, Adrian, Mitch, Justin, Dorothy, Deante, Auntie Betty, Horace, Chavonne, Erika, Patricia, Denetra, Brandon, Gemar, Nick, Uncle William, Uncle Leslie, Grandfather Julius, Robin, Tyler, Reggie, Tupac Shakur, Assata Shakur, Eldridge Cleaver, Ice Cube, Cypress Hill, Nas, Gil Scot Heron, Brian Jackson, Esham, Souls of Mischief, Donald Goines, Saafir, Charles Bukowski, Mike Tyson, The Roots, Mobb Deep, Ras Kass, Saul Williams, Common, Goodie Mob, Erykah Badu, and Organized Konfusion, I want to thank all of you in some kind of way for inspiring me, motivating me, believing in me, and hurting me. I definitely couldn't have written any of this without you.

Table of Contents

Vincent Vega..06

3 AM in Daytona Beach..07

Bloodshed & War..08

Resolution...09

Drama..10

Cheap Tequila Sunrise..12

Panhandle..14

Untitled..16

Everyday All Day..18

Santana's Party..20

Thinking in JAX International...21

Thursday, 7:45 PM..22

Friday, 1:15 AM..23

Sunday, 11:48 PM...24

Questions You Can't Ask..25

Walk Away..26

Same Old Thing Pt.2...27

Martha Street...28

Smack in the Face Pt.1..30

Hospice Room 630..31

Burn..32

Minnie..33

Dancer..34

Jasmyne Made Me Write This..35

De La Soul...36

The Routine……………………………………………………...............38

Untitled…………………………………………………………….....40

Repass…………………………………………………………….....41

An Honest Confession………………………………………….....42

Soul on Ice…………………………………………………….......43

Anger/Frustration………………………………………………......44

To Do List……………………………………………………….....45

Hire Me!……………………………………………………….......46

Laying in a Storm…………………………………………….......47

Thoughts While Drinking in Savannah……………………………....48

Basically……………………………………………………….....49

Direct Sale………………………………………………………......50

Same Old Thing Pt.3: The Muses………………………………....51

Watching Reruns of OZ………………………………………….....52

Love's Gonna Get You…………………………………………......54

Apartment Hunting…………………………………………….......55

Another One……………………………………………………......57

I'm Tired of Saying Their Names………………………………......58

A Memory from January…………………………………………....60

Gangster Rap from 1994……………………………………….......62

From July to Now……………………………………………….....64

9 Years down the Drain………………………………………….....66

Maintaining……………………………………………………....68

Vincent Vega

Leave the Interstate

Leave the cold air blowing outside the car

Leave reality

And just drive…

Press cruise control and ride out with the Isaac Hayes echo

Don't go….. Don't go….Don't go…. Don't go…

The look of love…

Now drift with Kendrick

You are…You are… a loner…loner.

Marijuana endorphins make you stronger…stronger

The destination is the alternate state of consciousness

You see, when you open your third eye.

No need to be high

Forget all of this around you

Forget your problems

Leave it all on Earth

And just drive

Fade away in the lights from the interstate

Get lost in Sade's voice

Your love is king, crown you with my heart

Your love is king, never need to part

Your kisses ring round and round and round my head

Touching the very part of me, making my soul sing

Just ride, but don't close your eyes.

3 AM in Daytona Beach

I am the night

Color me black

Dark as death on a one way street

All I have is a fist and a stone face

For the lost souls I greet

As it storms, a black hoodie covers my tears as I creep

The lyrics in my head guide me,

As I walk in search of some peace

Angels and Demons on my trail

Miles to go before I sleep.

Bloodshed & War

I awake with a scream

My spirit flew back into me

Tired of staying inside

So I let my mind ride free

So when you sleep

I creep

Armed with box cutters and brown Timberlands

I become Cain, forever walking the Earth

In search of self-worth

Cause it's a mosh pit up in my mind

Take your pick and see what you find

From Aliens, AK'S, Archangels, and Apocalypses

Triple sevens and triple sixes

Russian Roulette before you sleep

Thoughts cut deep

Like razors hidden in New York nightclubs

Absorb what I tell you

And take it in blood.

Resolution

Tonight I sleep alone

As I prepare to go back to hell in the morning

The voices get louder during the night

It's not fair that nobody else can hear them.

I cry out for help

But no one comes to answer

Especially her

She can fix everything, but chooses not to

I fell in love with a malicious mistress of madness

She causes havoc with black magic, leaving a trail of sadness

But enough of blaming her

I have to escape the prison of my mind alone

Embrace the darkness, that way it's not painful anymore

Now embrace the light so the healing can start

Happy to get that soul food for the mind

As well as the heart.

Drama

What's drama?

This is drama

Low GPA's

Hiding out from the days

Drinking away the pain

Wondering why you pray

You losing hope

Moms had a stroke

So many setbacks

No texts or call backs

Player haters

Senior papers

Of course it's that senior year stress

Where's the happiness?

You start to care less

Bum ass cars

Invisible scars, and shattering armor

What's drama?

That's drama

Mental illness

Sick of writing depressing shit

Lukewarm showers

And 120 credit hours

Box cutter blades

Thinking about the person you're supposed to hate

Some drama is big and some drama is small

But what you think is drama

Ain't even drama at all...

Cheap Tequila Sunrise

Boy I know you ain't hungover

There's nothing left in your body except carbon dioxide.

I know but still.

Still wishing I never got up off of that bathroom floor

The tiles were like silk.

The last thing you heard was drink this Aztec Gold

And don't be a bitch.

You ain't no bitch is you?

The next thing you see is the inside of the toilet bowl,

It's the cleanest one you ever seen.

So clean you hug that sucker

Too sick to sleep

Too tired to stay awake.

You gotta eat

I hate Wendy's and this bitch with the bad attitude

And worst hair weave makes the hate intensify.

I don't even want these nasty nuggets anymore

Give me some water

Nah don't even give me that.

Maybe you should smoke

Maybe you should drink some more

Maybe you should shut the hell up

Suck it up playboy

This is your first recovery day

The next one your ass gets, comes in May...

Panhandle

It never occurred to me that

Blue eyes could be so evil

I can tell that they've seen many changes over the years

From plantations to correctional facilities

They sing a song of hate

As they dance to the static of their walkie talkies

Simple things can have so much meaning in a place of madness

A hug

A smile

A card game

Looking in someone's eyes

The sound of someone's voice

The Great-Value version of Cinnamon Toast Crunch

To hold a hand for just a few moments is an eternity

Every letter in the words LOVE and APPRECIATION

Makes a thud inside of your head

Like a door that is controlled through bulletproof glass

I never knew a smile

Could break barbed wire

The sound of last call for canteen is muffled by laughter

We pretend to ignore it

We ignore those blue eyes

But you stand up

As the visiting area begins to clear

I'll see you next month cuz

When I'm not crying as I write this.

Untitled

Missing you.

Missing the idea of you

Missing you even

When I'm not missing you

Missing your voice

It changes its pitch in an instant

Missing your hair

And not just on your head

Your tattoos

The feel of your lips and your skin

These things can make hell feel like home

Missing your blunt wrappers

If I can find them

I can find you

Missing the liquor on your breath

You've been drinking overproof rum

I'm craving it

Missing the war between your legs

Missing your bed

I never knew how exhausted I was

Until I laid on it with you

Missing you asking me am I ok

When you know the answer

Missing every letter in your name

Missing you

Even when I shouldn't be missing you.

Everyday All Day

Never enough sleep

Never enough croissants in the morning

Never enough time to enjoy coffee

Never enough gas in the car

Never enough break time at work

Never enough money in my account

Never enough sneakers

Never enough tattoos

Never enough people whom

I want to call calling my phone

Never enough this one acting more like that one

Never enough that one acting more like that one

Never enough good thoughts

Never enough optimism

Never enough joy

Never enough pain

Never enough sunshine

Never enough rain

Never enough sex

Never enough pornos

Never enough lotion

Never enough sex

Never enough spirituality

Never enough God

Never enough prayer

Never enough words

Never enough rhymes

Never enough lyrics

Never enough tears

Never enough smiles

Never enough mood swings

Never enough I just don't want to be bothered

Never enough bring your ass over here and love me

When will never enough

Be just enough

Good enough

Well enough

Cause enough is enough.

Santana's Party

Led by a trail of ganja

I dance with jezebels

I smell the liquor on their breath

My fingers dominate their sundresses.

Their bodies cautiously being searched

Eyes blurry

Lungs roasted

Body numb

This is madness

But is welcomed

Then....

Time speeds back to normal

Feelings and sensations

Return like unwanted messages

The door closes

Leaving me out in the cold

Submitting to sobriety and loneliness

Again and again

Every weekend.

Thinking in JAX International

Why am I up at 1 when I have to be up at 8?

Why do I feel so out of place?

Out of shape

A waste of space

Why are my days going by on autopilot?

Inside, my head's a riot

A mosh pit with steel toe boots continually stomping

There has to be something better than this

Something better for me

A slave to my own rhythm

Waiting for the day that I'll be free.

Free from what?

Free from you

Free from me

I can't be around a bunch of people

Without wanting to swing at them

My anxiety rises and it's not surprising.

Thursday, 7:45 PM

Another one with pretty brown eyes

But when I look into them I see bold faced lies

Thought this one would bring the sunshine

Putting in work

Doing my dirt

And I'm the one that ends up getting hurt

The question remains why

I focus my energies into someone

Who's just another one of my enemies

Seeking to hurt me

Intentionally internally burning me like a bullet

And she's the one that pulled it.

I gotta stop looking for love to save me

Because I can't tell the difference between these vices and these ladies

Friday, 1:15 AM

My anger manifests in the form of blasting my car stereo

In nice neighborhoods

There is something like a 45 caliber bullet

Burning inside of me

And after nice sizes of Long Island ice teas,

I begin to piss on your sleep.

A Negro spiritual plays the role as my war drum.

I suffered through the years and shed so many tears

Lord I lost so many peers and shed so many tears.

My sadness becomes your misery

Do you hear me?

Do you see me?

You got something for this rage?

They say it's not healthy

You got something to make these tears come up out of me?

Because if I can't get peace because of her

You can't get peace because of me.

Sunday, 11:48 PM

In a garden of lust

A Poisonous fruit grows.

Eyes dilating with the sight of its wonders

Strawberry letters ripped into 23 pieces

Adrenaline flowing

The sun doesn't shine

Hallucinated rainbows and waterfalls

Leaking out of your mind

In this garden

I see

Pretty brown eyes staring back at me

I fly into of the arms

Of the one who owns them

And I am free.

Questions You Can't Ask

You're like a bullet in my head

Traveling throughout my brain

Picking spots to carve your name

Chicago White Sox hats can hide many things

Like scars, bumps, and crooked hair line-ups

But they don't hide pain

I wonder why you told so many lies

I wonder what I saw

When I looked you dead in your eyes

What happened to caring for me?

What happened to Mortal Kombat in HD?

What happened to dancing for me?

Walk Away

What happened to you and me?

What ever happened to the two of us?

Two brothers against an entire army?

The lyricist and the DJ

The right and the left hand

We swore that together

We would be the masters of our very own realities

But now you can't even look at me

And can't even answer why now we are enemies.

You forgot about me

But still I wish you peace.

Same Old Thing Pt.2

Love got my mind tripping

Its heart ripping

Spirit slipping

Cause I'm steady wishing

I hear the dancer calling

My hope is falling

Like its tenth grade all over again

Damn

Her brown eyes has me encased in this box again

Where's the love at?

She left me with none of that.

I'm just a stupid motherfucker

I can't believe I let her drag my spirit in the gutter.

Martha Street

Random Cars cruise towards the oncoming ramp.

Police sirens ring out into the night like Banshees.

Gunshots march out into the street in a cadence

They move north towards their freedom.

The wind blows outside my window

It cries out Erika.

Drunks lash out against an unknown enemy

But it is a war of no concern. So it seems

Samurai Champloo lounges in the background,

Waiting to be watched after Daredevil.

I think binge watching it

Has given me his heightened senses.

Lying in darkness

Hearing more bullets

My mind starting to fade

Wishing I was faded

The wind becomes bitter.

Erika is not coming

Bullets march closer

Shell casings chant as they dance on concrete

Drunks get louder as a bottle shatters,

Their enemy is winning this battle

Every night their wars move closer.

It is clear to me

By the glass on the street the next morning

That this is a dispute between a broken mind and MD 20/20

The mad dog is winning

It always does.

Smack in the Face Pt. 1

Love got my mind tripping

Caught me slipping

Steady dipping in my accord wishing this was a bad dream.

But it seems this is the accurate reality

Used to roll deep with a crew

But what do you do

When the only one in your crew now is you?

Am I blue...?

Waking from this dream

I see I can trust no man from now until infinity.

You're either my brother

Or just consider yourself my enemy

Enemies

Scheming on stealing my energy

And that's all that surrounds me.

What can I do?

Behind enemy lines and ain't nobody to run to.

My mind is playing tricks on me so don't play with me

Did I really diss all my homies

Because I'm feeling kind of lonely

Slowly they all act like they don't know me.

Hospice Room 630

You ready for the Lord boy?

I'm trying to get ready Granddaddy.

I know you spy the daze in my eyes

Look to the skies

The Lord is coming for his prize.

I hear my brothers calling me to come on

I ain't ready to go yet so they got to run on

I ain't dead

I'm getting up out of this bed.

I believe you gonna remember me not as what you see

Not as this cancer is enslaving me

Not stuck up with all these I.V's

This geechie blood evaporating

Nurses touching on me

I believe you gonna remember me not as what you see.

Burn

This heat is gonna bash words out of my head

Whether I want them to come out or not

With no air conditioning I swim in my own emotions

Fighting their currents as they crash onto the rocks of reality.

Caught in a rapture as Cypress Hill's Temples of Boom loops continuously

As I wander aimlessly lost in a hail of hunger

Boredom, addiction, and disappointment.

My brain is on its ashy knees

Begging for answers to questions repeatedly asked

Where is the alcohol?

Where is the rain?

Where is my money?

Why does she want my heart all of a sudden?

Why did she stop texting me after I sent her song lyrics?

Why is it 97 degrees?

Who said the world was gonna end today?

I have bathed in the apocalypse

Soaking myself in the why

Praying for the what

Too proud to ask for the where

But bold enough to try and steal the when

When do I win?

When does it end?

Minnie

Anything can trigger a memory

They manifest on an instant

A smell

A saying

Even bread pudding

Can resurrect a scenario

A person

Who has long faded away

As I sit in a house

Filled with beer

And Vodka

And Gumbo

Miles away from my reality

Inside of a house that someone would break into

There are more differences than similarities

Of course vanilla extract and the cinnamon

She used Jack Daniels

This woman uses Jim Beam

Is there a difference between toasted Wheat bread and French bread?

I have to stop this now

Because I can't eat, cry, and write at the same time.

Dancer

This is for my niece

She's a young warrior

A lioness

Tomorrow is her birthday

She'll be 7 years old

Love is all around you

You know it's there

You can feel it

Even if you can't see it

And a child shall lead them to places

They couldn't bring themselves to go

How can a child's smile

Make the devil inside of you die for a little while?

Jasmyne Made Me Write This

Go away cat

You make me smile too much

Beautiful Sundays set off the love train.

It moves every second of every hour

Passing through a field of sunflowers

Unhappy for so many days

Wishing my life would end in so many ways

But something is holding my spirit

There's so much love inside of me

And I never knew until now of its feeling.

Joy and pain

Is like sunshine and rain

Joy and pain

Is like sunshine and rain

Days like this

Make lyrics like this

They better

Stay like this

Because I got so much love to give

It's ridiculous that now I want to live.

De La Soul

Mess up my mind

They got me in a daze

Mess up my mind

Mess up my mind

They got me in a daze

Look in the mirror

And what do you see?

A piece of shit staring back at me.

Thinking of opening up my Quran and Bible

Keep the devils out my mind because it's idle

The world spins and I wonder why that boy lied.

Said he was my brother till the day he died

Nowadays we don't even speak.

It seems like everyone is an enemy

Or wants a favor from me

Show love to these people but who shows love to me?

Left without a clue

What can I do?

I choose to escape in the rays of the burning sun

And feel the wind from a sandy shore

Moving close to the water

So it pulls me out

Until you can't see my dreads no more.

Mess up my mind

Mess up my mind

You got me in a daze

Mess up my mind

Mess up my mind

She got me in a daze

Mess up my mind

Mess up my mind

He got me in a daze

Mess up my mind

Mess up my mind

Even I got me in a daze

The Routine

Get up fool

You're not dead yet

So its work to be done

Sit on your bed for 5 minutes exactly

Put your clothes on that you didn't iron

Wash the anxiety off of your face

Brush your teeth. Your tongue too.

It's not even 9 o'clock yet

But answer your mother's questions with half answers

Trust me she'll shut up

Walk out the door

It'll be a scorcher today

So you pray for rain

Pray this ain't the day your car stops working

Just pray period

If God is up there he'll get the message

Or maybe half of it at least

Walk in McDonald's

The cashier knows what you want

But you gotta tell him anyway

Large coffee 7 creams and 12 sugars

Pay your $1.49

Throw the receipt away

And wonder why it's $1.49 when it used to be $1.07

Pull into work and listen

As your phone plays a song that should be played

When anxiety and anger sings off key in unison.

Take two sips of the coffee

Take a deep breath

Turn the car off

Open the door

Start walking fool

You're not dead yet.

Untitled

Hard to breathe like a bullet in the lungs

Imbalances of chemicals in my brain

Create a paranoia agent

All in the area is negative energy

And it's all swinging at me

In this place I sit quiet

But internally I start a riot

Brother you've got to calm down

Says that voice again

Forget that.

I can see I'm what these people around despise

By the look in their eyes

Like 7:36 am my anger starts to rise

I rhyme back

They're not paying you any attention

He says

Liar! I ain't crazy I retort

Come on brother, chill out.

Now get up and walk out of the building

There you go

Get some air

There you go homie.

Just breathe,

Just breathe, just.....breathe.

Repass

My mind races

At Mach 5 speeds

Thumps in my head so intense

I become the living embodiment of a stereo system

You gotta get some air

A voice says

I'm already outside

Well you got to get some liquor then

The voice says back

Vodka and pink lemonade

Has just got to heal these wounds I can't see right?

It doesn't …

It fails to blur out these faces that keep saying

You held your mother down today

What else was I supposed to do?

There is not much that can be done in this predicament

So I'll ride out into the night

No cd's playing

No A/C blowing

Just me and the aroma of alcohol and death that lounges in the air.

An Honest Confession

I know that I'm not in love with you anymore

How you ask?

Well of course my heart rate

Doesn't increase when you come around

The live version of Lately by Jodeci

Doesn't resonate as much

I don't get physically exhausted

Whenever the thought of you enters my head

Clearly I'm not a good liar….

Soul on Ice

It is blasphemy to think of you

But I do it faithfully

I feel your energy 500 miles away

You are my demon

But I am not afraid of you

The words I keep telling myself

As I look you dead in your eyes

You have fragments…Chunks of me

And I would like to have them back

The resolution we must meet

Will lead us to the Apocalypse

Archangels will appear

To stop this affection that will not rest in peace

There is no other way.

We all have to deal with our demons one day…..

Anger/Frustration

I've got to Malcolm Exorcise this demon out of me

This anger I got ain't good for my health

I'm sure, absolute like vodka

Read this rage I published on every page

And come up with a dissertation

For why I keep losing my patience with these mortals

I sense they're trying me

Fantasies of me smashing them

Like a Holocaust survivor when he spots a Neo-Nazi

Only the powers of light can stop me

And absorb this negative energy

God if you listening help me

Cause I got enough of this to aim at you

I'm thinking how I feel is somewhat entertaining for you

Forgive me lord I have sinned

But you see all these emotions I'm drowning in

And without a lifeboat I need some hope

Internally I burn with 21 years of hellfire

Regardless if I use it to my advantage

It burns my soul so bad I can't stand it

So God I pass it to you,

I bet money you can manage…

To Do List

Gotta learn to stop caring about people

Who care nothing for me

Gotta learn how to forgive

Just like I learned how to never forget

Gotta learn how to not call my therapist all the time

And I gotta learn to call my therapist to let her know I'm alright.

Gotta learn to lace my prayers with sincerity

Instead of anger and frustration

Gotta learn how to not be afraid of someone loving me back

Just like I ain't afraid of a bullet.

Gotta learn how to take care of my heart and my soul,

Because both of them are gonna take care of me.

Gotta learn how to get my hair to fit in hats

Without the hat falling off

Gotta learn how to fix my grandmother's record player

So I can buy Dr. Dre's The Chronic on vinyl

And gotta learn fast...

Hire Me!

I've been looking for jobs. Well kind of.

Finding a job basically is a bloody job,

But most of the time I ask myself do I really want a job,

Or just want the money?

Plus in my opinion I got plenty of damn jobs.

For instance,

Trying to stay nappy headed when everyone says be clean cut is a job

Not getting a drink when every day I want to drink is a job

Watching people watch me

Or at least I think they're watching me

Whenever I walk into a store is a job.

Fixing my resume without pasting a picture of me

On my knees on it is a fucking job

Thinking about people

Who I'm pretty sure aren't thinking about me is a job

Trying to believe the tarot reader

While at the same time wondering why the hell

I am even listening to a tarot reader is a job.

Jobs

Jobs all around me except they just ain't paying...

Laying in a Storm

Still afraid

Still on guard

But please don't stop loving on me

Touching on me

I gotta leave

I think you scheme to destroy me

You've done it before

So you wanna do it some more?

You make my insides burn

Like they're filled with Hennessy.

And it's all because you care for me.

Thoughts While Drinking in Savannah

Looking in her pretty brown eyes

All I can see is bold face lies

Here I lay robbed of my patience

Because here I am frolicking with the devils maiden.

It's becoming harder to trust you

Something about you is corrupt

I can sense it when I touch you

It's a shame, whenever you say my name energy surges my brain

A Sorceress mixing potions that induce childlike emotions

Unbelievable

My enemy is the same one making me smile.

Basically

Happiness

Is not something you buy

You steal

Not something you borrow

Not something you drink too much of

Not something you smoke

Not something you ingest

Not something you inject

Not something you listen to

Not something you etch on your skin

Not something you get from someone else

Not something you get an orgasm from

Not something you put in a collection plate

It's something you create

And for many creators

Especially writers

Well writers such as myself

This is a hard concept to grasp.

Because it's very hard

To create something you know nothing about.

Direct Sale

Rubber burns

As thunder cracks

Suspense fills the air

As heatwaves submit to lightning

Darkness opens its legs on a murky canvas

Rainfall is looming in the distance

A door opens

A voice calls out as more darkness greets me

It's hard to tell if I'm talking to my uncle or his demon

The God of White Dreams

Addicts have offered sacrifices to him for centuries

His fingerprints are everywhere on his body

From the sniffles to the fast talking

As the lightning dances in the house

It spotlights the bags under his eyes

The thunder rings out like automatic gunfire

As I give what he asks for.

More sniffles and stutters

Are chased by promises of repaid debts.

The door opens again

The rain is waiting

Lightning dances once more

As the night sets the stage for the god to rule once more.

Same Old Thing Pt.3: The Muses

Never date a woman with the letter A

At the end of her first name

Patricia places me in purgatory

I pray for absolution from Erika

And Tashima completes the trinity

There are many stories to be told about these three

I have tasted liquor on their tongues

Grinded to the rhythms of their bodies

And drowned in illusions of my own creation

While looking into their eyes

I have taken a bite of their spirits

And have both vomited and craved more.

Entire energies have been presented to them

And had been repaid with the touch of a stranger

And the eyes of an executioner.

They leave anger, confusion and misery in their wake

Making one seek refuge into the arms of alcohol and ink pens.

This is the price that is paid when you sow seeds of love

And a poisonous fruit is the reaping.

Watching Reruns of OZ

I am a man

My dreams are illegal

But I push them regardless

On a daily basis I wait for God

And hear the devil

I dance in the wind and rain

I curse the sun

A person of many hats

I'm a brutalizer

I'm a bitch

I fantasize about getting killed

And I fantasize about getting kissed

My hair is nappy

My shoes are overpriced and dirty

My pants sag (out of my workplace)

My body is etched in ink

I am a man

I like my women tall

And with the eyes of witches

My liquor strong

Sweet and standing on my stomach

My money in both 4 to 6

Odd and even numbers

And my love loving me back

I am a man

Straight like that.

Love's Gonna Get You

When I love

I LOVE.

Love you to death

To life

Down to your dirty drawers

If you're wrong

If you're right

At 10 o'clock in morning

At 3 o'clock at night

I love when love don't show up on time

When it tells bold face lies

When it owes me money

When it acts funny

Hell, I even love when love don't love.

I love so much that I think about love even

When I know love ain't thinking about me

If I love you

I love you even when I'm not loving you

Whether you my brother

Or if I'm kissing you

Love stays on my mind

So I'll love every time

With every rhyme

All the time.

Apartment Hunting

I have dreams of moving out of my mother's house

It would be grand

When I come in the house

No one would ask me about how the day was

No one would ask me questions

If they couldn't get in

Yeah the independence is great

But I would get to walk around my place naked!

Why?!?!

Cause it's my place that's why!

I pay the rent here

When people come over and tell me that I overpaid

And that their place is bigger than mine

I would tell them that they could always go back to their place

Matter of fact

I would tell them in the exact way

Martin Lawrence does on his show

My anxiety

A large poster of Tupac Shakur

And Incense

Would greet my guests at the door

And the ambiance would scream don't get too comfortable

And eat before you come over here at them.

Ah, it would be grand.

Another One

It is very frightening to wake up in the morning

And watch the news

And be resigned to the fact that the skin you have

Which is seen as a source of magic and power

But there are other powers around you

That desire to add bullets to this said skin

I can tell you from personal experience that

Bullets burn...

I'm Tired of Saying Their Names

I never told another man

Well at least one around my age

That I loved him

Until I walked around with him

And the eyes that were fixated on him

Watched him carefully

As if they were in the presence of a demon

Until I saw one man that looked like him dead in the street

That the bullets which riddled his body were justified

Because he looked as if he could be a threat to some imaginary innocence

I never told another man

That I loved him

Until I witnessed firsthand that a complexion

Mixed with testosterone

Could be a death sentence.

When I could do nothing but chant his name

When his enemies saw his crown before he did

And proceeded to snatch it from him

With his head still attached.

I never told another woman

Well at least one around my age

That I loved her

Until I watched her look into a mirror

And then beat at it until her hands were bloodied

Until demons mocked her appearance and then stole it from her

When I knew she had the potential to construct an entire universe

But watched as she was programmed to hate her creations

When I could do nothing but chant her name

When her enemies shackled and destroyed her

And then looked me in my face

And told me that she destroyed herself.

How can I say I loved them?

When I couldn't protect them?

A Memory from January

One time in St. Petersburg

I was staying with some friends of mine.

They were having a few people over for drinks

And to play Taboo of all things.

I paid them no attention as

I found Nelson Mandela's book Long Road to Freedom

Beside a second season of True Blood

Right when it started to get interesting

My friend Aaron yells

Boy put that book down!"

All these white people about to come over here

And you're reading about Mandela!

Plus you've been drinking already too!

He snatches the book and throws it into another room

Everybody laughs

I do too

I'm trying not to be seen as the angry black guy anymore.

Later on that night

I sit on the couch watching but not watching

The others play video games.

There were my friends who I came with

And my hosts boyfriend

Who was Egyptian sitting in a sea of white folks

I meant to say

"Well this must be the colored folks section."

In my head

But my mouth said it aloud

Luckily I happened to get a few laughs.

Especially from the Egyptian.

It was then he challenged me

To see how many shots of tequila I could take.

I was challenged so I had to oblige.

The next thing I remember

Is a familiar hand holding my hair

As my face was in the toilet.

Another familiar voice kept asking me to move over

But I couldn't make out what else they said.

The next morning

I was challenged again to another drink.

I had to oblige

I was challenged.

I wish I remembered what page I was on though.

Gangster Rap from 1994

Mr. Blue is inside of you

Never lie

Do or die

Bring tears to your eyes

Run and hide

The soul taker

The player hater

Induce sleep

From my style of misery

Feel me in your stomach and your chest

I'm a high caliber slug

Show no love

Keeping that piss poor look on your face

You a fucking disgrace

Anxiety mixed with me

Makes everyone your enemy

No drug or drink can step to me

Even sex is inferior weaponry

I'm your personal demon

Got you screaming your bloody head off

Shit on your mind

You got to get off

Lit the fuse

And look what went off.

When your homies dip

Mr. Blue stays fucking with you

The feeling you got when old girl dropped you

I sprayed you with mace

Got you hiding your tears

As a dozen roses smile right in your face.

From July to Now

I often think of you

Well the idea of you.

You wore a lot of bright colors

But you wore them well

I adored you.

Still do

I remember your living room

And how it looked like my living room

The picture of your sister

And the picture of you when you were younger.

I remember the VCR tapes in your room

You weren't lying when you said you didn't watch TV

The picture of the Tiger in your room

Reminded me of you for some reason

Graceful... Mysterious... Elegant.

Maybe I should blame Schoolboy Q

For why you stopped talking to me

I guess you didn't like his lyrics

Its fine I guess. I understand

(No it's not. I don't understand.)

I've been meaning to call you

But things keep happening

Like my anxiety tells me not to

My phone is on 5 percent when I pump myself up to do it

I got high and forgot

Something tells me I'm gonna get your voicemail

I got high and forgot

Someone is telling me to let the idea of you go

I got high and forgot

But every time I come down

You're still inside of my head

Smiling

Wearing bright colors

And rolling your eyes at me.

9 Years down the Drain

Yesterday I walked in the Urban Outfitters store

I had an urge to buy a shirt that would be

32 dollars after tax

In the corner of my eye

I see my former best friend.

I forgot he works in the store part time.

Move quickly so he doesn't notice you

Is this shirt really worth it?

Yes, it has Tupac on it

And I've wanted it for 3 months.

As he heads to the back of the store

I head to the line

Less than two minutes later

He is standing on the peripheral

I turn and look at him

He looks like somebody else

Somebody I would laugh at

If I saw them in the street

A sucker

He makes a joke about how

I've been selected as for a random search.

I wish it hadn't come to this

I can't help the smile on my face as it turns into contempt

As I say to him "Fuck you nigga"

And turn back around towards the cash register.

He is gone when I look behind me again

I'm not even supposed to be in here

Sorry Tupac, but you're not coming home with me today.

Maintaining

Your brothers have buried you

As you offered allegiance

They repaid with blasphemy

You have sat at a lovers table and eaten their lies.

Adoration has been replaced by Anarchy

Thought patterns have terrorized the heavens

In response to unanswered prayers

You have carried the anger of 10000 slaves

But in the process of this

You have only allowed bitterness to shackle your spirit

The earth spins

The liquor pours

The sun curses

The rain dances

And you are still here.

About the Writer

He was always taught by his mother to not be quiet and to speak his mind. He still never did speak too much, but he definitely used pens, paper, and sometimes microphones to express himself. Rashad Hawkins was born Joshua Rashad Hawkins, on April 10th 1992, and hails from Jacksonville, Florida. He is a Freelance Writer and aspiring Blogger. Rashad had always been known as a writer to his family, always creating short stories and comic book characters. He had always wanted to become a professional basketball player, however at the age of 10 his interests immediately changed when he wrote his first poem during a horrible summer staying at one of his aunt's house. After attending Douglas Anderson School of The Arts for Creative Writing, he attended Bethune-Cookman University where he received a Bachelor's Degree in Mass Communication with an emphasis in Journalism. It was here that he was a staff writer on the school newspaper The Voice of the Wildcats, and was published in Daytona Beach News Journal. His poems have also been published in two anthologies: Kindling Literary Anthology Vol.1 (2013) and Kindling Literary Anthology Vol.2 (2014). Many of his works are inspired by his life experiences, music, various soliloquies, and personal relationships.